VENEZUELAN CLIMBS

Stephen Platt

www.leveretpublishing.com

Venezuelan Climbs
First published - October 2025
Published by Leveret Publishing
56 Covent Garden, Cambridge, CB1 2HR, UK

Pemón indian food - casava, fish stew, chilli and cachire

ISBN 978-1-912460-76-2

© Stephen Platt 2025

All rights reserved. No part of this publication may be reproduced, stored in a retrieval system or transmitted in any form by any means, electronic, mechanical, photocopying, recording or otherwise, except brief extracts for the purpose of review, without the written permission of the publisher.

VENEZUELAN CLIMBS

Preamble

We lived in Venezuela for five years when the children were young, from 1970 to 1975. I was working in the art school in Manchester, in the School of Advanced Studies. I liked my job as a junior lecturer, and I liked my boss, Ray Gray, an industrial designer.

Alberto, a student on the Master's course I'd done the previous year., invited us to dinner to meet fellow Venezuelan students and their wives. He talked about Venezuela and the opportunities there, and said he could get me a job with his uncle, Manuel, who was head of urban planning. He described how towns were growing and needed a town plan to unlock investment. I told him I didn't know anything about planning. Alberto said it didn't matter. I was just what Manuel needed in his department's socio-economic unit. I didn't take the offer seriously,. I was just getting back into serious climbing in the UK and I wasn't sure what climbing opportunities there would be in Venezuela. But in the morning, Dorothea, said, Let's go. She had been born and brought up in Manchester and was sick and tired of childcare, wanting a taste of adventure.

In Venezuela I went to the Ministry and met Manuel. He said that they had run out of money for the year and couldn't pay me. He suggested I come back in March or April. I said that wasn't possible, as we'd sold up and the family were due to arrive by ship. I started work anyway.. I found a flat, the family arrived, but all our possessions, including my climbing gear, had gone missing on the voyage. Somehow, with a small loan from Alberto's mother, Mildred, we managed. Our landlord, the local grocery store and the Institute, where I went to Spanish classes every night, generously agreed to trust me to pay them back.

At first I knew hardly anyone. Alberto and the Venezuelans I met in England were still there, and before the internet, it wasn't that easy to get connected or know if there was any climbing. I began exploring, walking on the Avila with Jerry, whom I'd met at Spanish classes. After 6 months our possessions turned up in in the port of La Guiara, I started to meet other climbers; David Nott, Ramon and Hans. The following recounts some of our adventures.

Cerro El Avila

November 1970 - November 1975

We moved to Venezuela in September 1970 and our first flat was in Las Palmas at the foot of the Avila, the mountain chain that forms a barrier between the Valley of Caracas and the Caribbean coast. My first view of the Avila was from the air as I flew along the coast from Trinidad; a green wilderness with no sign of civilisation, no buildings or roads to be seen, just mountainous forest until we began the descent into Maicatia airport.

Cerro El Avila is the 80 km mountain range that rises to 9000 feet between the valley of Caracas at 3000 feet and the Caribbean coast. The uplift of gneiss and schist rock was formed relatively recently in the Tertiary age, about 60 million years ago. Although close to the capital and with plenty of hiking trails, parts of the mountains are wild and challenging and home to diverse wildlife, including howler monkey, snakes, jaguar, and many species of exotic birds.

El Avila, from nearby our flat in Avenida Amazonas

I began walking on the Avila with Jerry, a young American I met at Spanish classes in the Centro Venezolano Americano in Las Mercedes. We arranged to meet early on Sunday morning at the Cota Mil, the Avenida Boyacá that runs along the base of the mountain. The first bit of a concrete road up to the Sabas Nieves Guardia Parques was ridiculously steep, and my carves ached with the effort, and I struggled to keep up. We reached the fire break that circles the mountain and the road became a path. It was steep, but contouring with the slope, so easier on the legs. The park guardian's hut is an oval-shaped metal cabin with a dome roof. The Guardian asked us to sign his book. Jerry told me his twin brother was the Guardian at Sebucan and had a proper house, which had caused bad feelings.

We passed Loma Serrano, a grassy knoll surrounded by eucalyptus trees that tinkled in the breeze. I would have liked to stop, but Jerry wanted to press on, as he was timing our ascent. We reached la Silla de Caracas, the wide col on the Fila Maestra, and proceeded along the ridge to Pico Oriental. The vegetation was open, scrub and coarse grasses, frailejones and monster heather. Jerry said he liked this route because it was more

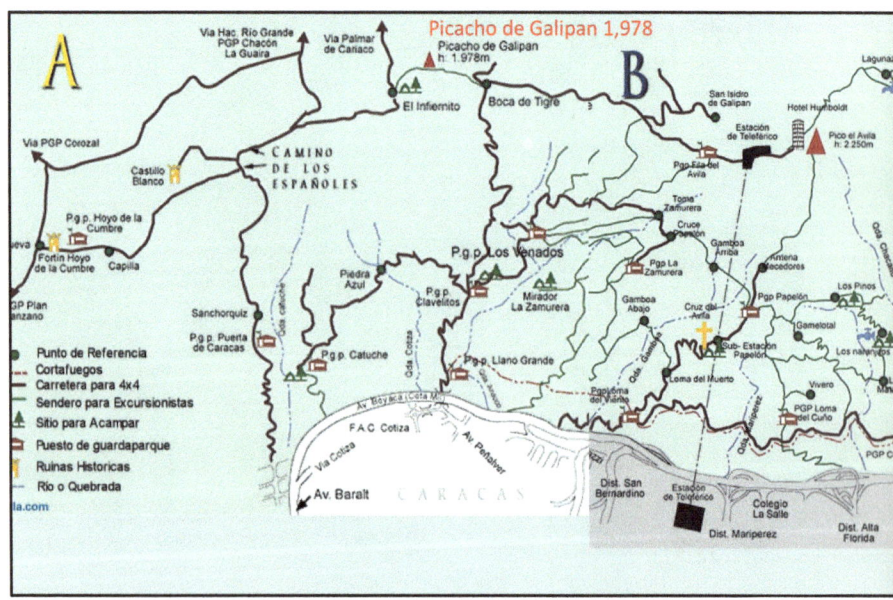

Hotel Humboldt, Avila

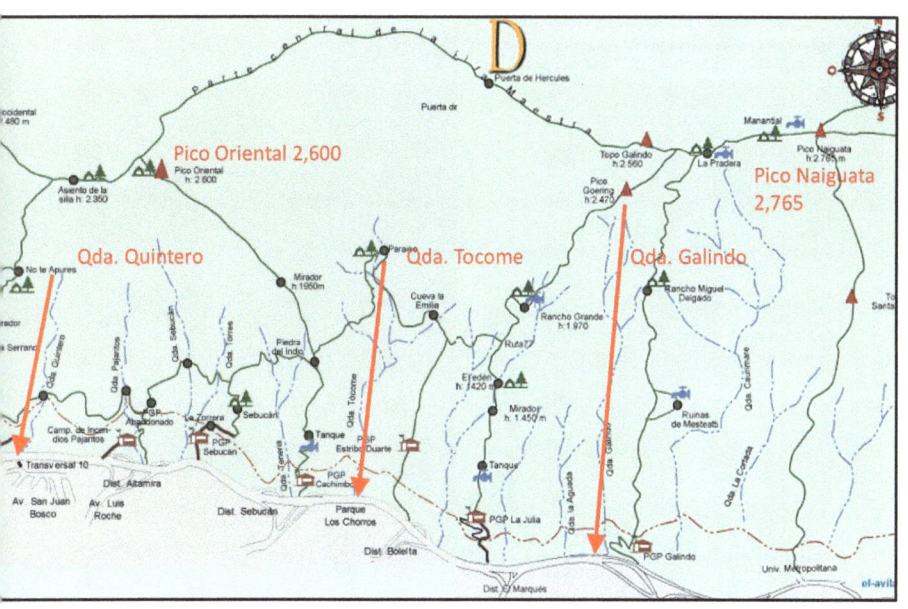

Pico Naiguata

Steve snoozing after climbing Pico Oriental

open, there were fewer dangerous snakes, and he was used to it. I looked along the length of the chain and realised that the mountain held areas of forest and canyons with waterfalls, and that parts would be much wilder than the route we'd followed.

We'd been living in Venezuela for over six months when our belongings turned up. We got a call from La Guaira, the port, that the two boxes that came with the family on the boat from England had been found. By then I had been paid, and we had bought a car, a Wileys jeep. We went to fetch them, but they were too big to fit in the jeep, so we hired two big old American taxis to take them. The boxes were so heavy, sticking out of the boots that the front wheels risked lifting off the ground. We unloaded them in the parking lot under our apartment. One of the boxes broke open, and thousands of cockroaches ran out and scattered across the concrete and disappeared. One of the boxes contained my climbing gear, ropes, boots and slings.

I repeated the Sabas Nieves route various times with Jerry, but began to explore further afield, including Pico Oriental from Cachimbo and I persuaded Jerry to explore the Quebrada Tocomé, one of the many steep

Ramon and youths from Centro Excursionista Caracas

Quebrada Quintero

river gorges flowing down the mountain to the city. By then I'd met David Nott. David was an English journalist reporting on Latin American economies, and he was married to a Venezuelan living in Caracas. I had heard he was a climber, and Dorothea and I arranged to go and meet him and his wife, Mariella, at the cinema in Chacaito. David was 10 years older than me. Mariella was most vivacious, had studied architecture at the University of Caracas and worked in an advertising agency. David invited me to explore a Quebrada Quintero and abseil down. We went somewhere low down on the mountain near the fire-break.

Despite its obvious limitations, it gave me the idea that one or more of the bigger quebradas would pose a challenge. So I persuaded Jerry to come with me to El Paraiso from where we'd be able to descend the Quebrada Tocomé. This was the large quebrada with waterfalls I could see from our apartment across the valley. To get to El Paraiso, you climb towards Pico Oriental, and then traverse east along a good path that is increasingly forested.

El Paraiso is a beautiful spot where the path crosses a stream. The water is shallow and I began rock hopping, but soon resigned myself to getting

Cascada El Paraiso, Quebrada Tocomé

Quebrada Tocomé

wet and started wading. The descent got steeper and we slid down a tree trunk into a pool. We rigged up an abseil around a tree at a bigger drop, and I went first, sinking into deep water before swimming across to the bank. Jerry followed, but got tangled in the ropes and started drowning. I dove back in and dragged him out. I can't swim, he spluttered. I fine time to tell me now I thought.

The canyon narrowed and we reached a huge fall where my rope was too short. There were rock walls on either side of us and no way back up the fall that we'd just abseiled down. There was no alternative but to try to climb up the side wall. It was hard, and I had to trust a pull on a liana

Quebrada Tocomé

root to get up, We got back in the dark. I tried again with David Nott, but we got trapped again lower down as the light gave out and had to climb out again. I finally made it all the way down with Vivian. David's son, a fireman, who was over on a visit. I did the quebrada a number of times – once with my son, Jonathan, who was only eight at the time, once with Chino and Marianti, who did it in bare feet, and with Scharlie on our visit in 1981, I even went with Daniel and his Swiss filmmaker friend to make a film of the descent. It took three days, and we slept in hammocks, listening to the hooting of howler monkeys.

I had seen a cliff about 150 feet high from the highway at the base of the Avila, and conceived the idea to try to climb it. I'd seen some steel reinforcing rods at an abandoned building site, and I pinched two suitable lengths. I climbed to the top of the crag by a path at the side and traversed to the top of the cliff. I felt around in the grass to find a crack or opening of some kind in the rock, and banged in the steel rods at least a foot. I attached the rope and abseiled down, inspecting the rock as I went. The section above the overhang was steep, almost a wall, but there were small holes. The overhang would be difficult, but there seemed to be a way. The lower section was devoid of holes, but was a slab, and I felt

Jonathan, Ramon and people from Excursionista Club

Upper wall of Cota Mile, Steve

Cota Mile, Steve and Hans on lower slab

Ramon on Cotal Mil traverse

confident I'd be able to climb it.

I hung my sack on the end of the rope to weight it down and ensure it hung vertically. Then I tied a prusik loop to the rope and started up. It wasn't as good as top roping with a partner holding the rope, but I hoped it would hold me if I fell. The overhang was the most challenging part, featuring a layaway hold and a high step. I managed it, but then I had to be careful to locate the holes on the upper wall without falling. I used to go to the cliff on Saturday or Sunday mornings. I also did the semi-circular traverse under the overhang. The holes were extremely small, and the drop got higher and higher as one reached the centre of the crag, before reducing as one reached the opposite side. I had a tricky time passing a wasp nest near the highest point. Sentinels left the hanging stalk of a nest and buzzed around my head. I had to remain very still and move gently to avoid the swarm emerging and attacking me. I wasn't sure I'd be able to avoid falling off if I was stung badly. I had to use holds within a foot of the nest and glide past, hoping for the best by moving slowly and smoothly. I got past safely and made it across.

I had been there a few times when two people arrived and introduced themselves as climbers – Ramon Blanco and Hans Schwarzer. They said they were going rock climbing. They were the first climbers I'd met, and I was keen to find out more about them. I pointed to the cliff behind me, but they didn't seem interested and they set off up the hillside. I pulled down the ropes, packed as quickly as I could, and followed them. I caught up with them at a small rock called the Piedra del Indio, where they had started climbing. I wasn't very impressed with the rock, so I persuaded them to try my cliff. We became friends, and did a lot of climbing together on the Avila, the Gran Savanna, San Juan de los Moros, the Sierra Nevada de Merida, Mexico and Ecuador. I did the Pico Oriental various times with Ramon and he was very fast. The three of us did the Pueblo to Porto route, an amazing traverse along the central Avila Ridge, from the Puerta de Caracas in the west to the Porto de Naiguata on the coast, a distance of over 25 miles of difficult terrain.

We set off early in the morning and walked all day. I remember I didn't take enough water or food, and Ramon and Hans were better organised than I was, but they didn't share their nice bread and cheese. I also camped on the summit of Pico Naiguata with Jonathan. But the most fantastic trip I did on the Avila was with Ramon descending Quebrada Galindo from the Fila Maestra. It nearly killed us.

Jonathan and friend on summit of Pico Naiguatá

Camping on summit Pico Naiguatá

Quebrada Galindo

Quebrada Galindo

We began early, but the quebrada was so long that night caught us still some way from the bottom in a near-vertical, narrow chute. I had descended first, and the rope ran out. I was perched in a slight depression in the fall where there was a level area about a yard square before the falls continued downwards. I couldn't find a belay. I couldn't see in the pitch dark, and could hardly think with the crashing of the water. Ramon started descending. There was no way he could have heard me shouting not to come. He crouched in the back of the chute behind the main torrent, and I shouted into his ear that I couldn't find a belay. Amazingly, despite the noise and the danger he was dropping off to sleep. My teeth were chattering and I was shaking with cold. It was freezing, and I was soaking wet, and there was a cold wind blowing up the falls. I still couldn't find a belay but we couldn't climb back up the rope that was hanging free. I have never felt so terrified. I didn't know what to do, and Ramon was no help. I felt around in the pool at my feet and found a rock about the size of a concrete block. The lip of the chute narrowed before plunging down. I

Los Chorros, base of Quebrada Galindo

knew we were near the bottom because I could hear traffic above the roar of the water, I somehow conceived the crazy plan of using the rock in the narrow lip of the chute, like a chock stone, to anchor the ropes.

I pulled the ropes down, threading them around the stone, and let the current carry the rope over the lip. I hung on for dear life, trying to stop it from slipping out of my grip. I shouted in Ramon's ear to come when he felt the ropes go slack, and gingerly lowered myself over the edge. I was hanging and twisting in space with the water crashing over me. I expected the rock to dislodge, but amazingly, it held. I seemed to descend forever,

Picacho de Galipan

and I wondered if the ropes would be long enough. I couldn't see anything, and then I was down on the ground, flat earth beneath my feet. What a relief. Then Ramon was descending safely. We gently pulled on the rope, expecting to have to dodge the falling chock stone, but it held, and the ropes came down cleanly, and we were home free with only a short walk through the forest and along the Cota Mil back to the car.

The Picacho de Galipan is the biggest rock face on the Avila. It's at the western end of the ridge, and can be reached either from the teleferico or by the the dirt road across the mountain from Cotiza to the coast. I went to climb it with David. We had to force our way through the thick undergrowth to reach the base of the rock. The cliff is a steep slab just off vertical, and holdless. It was also devoid of any natural protection, where I could place running belays. I could see a small ledge at about 120 feet up, and made for it. The climbing was very thin, with little for the hands or feet, and no positive holds, just flakes and wrinkles.

I breathed a sigh of relief on getting my hands on the ledge and moved up with the idea of mantle shelving when I came face to face with a large snake. It was basking there and doing no one any harm. I was about a foot

Ramon, Hans, Wolfi and ANO below Picacho de Galipan

away from it, and we eyed each other. It could have bitten me in the face, but it didn't. I didn't know what to do. I could climb onto the ledge and perhaps knock the snake off, but I was likely to be bitten, or I could go back down. But reversing the pitch I just climbed seemed impossible. I had no runners to protect me if I fell, and I found it hard, climbing up. Going back down, unable to see the holds from my feet, would be even harder. The snake, from photographs I'd seen, was most likely a deadly Tigra Mariposa. If it bit me, I'd have to get down somehow, anyway. So gingerly and slowly, I lowered down out of sight of the snake. All this perhaps took two or three seconds. I shouted I was coming down, and very slowly and carefully, began to descend. I got down safely. I returned another time with Ramon Hanson Wolfie, but they wouldn't tackle the main cliff face, and we climbed up a vegetated ridge to the side.

After Scharlie and I climbed, Treman Tepui, Wilmer invited us to go with him to Galipan to hang glide. He told me about hang gliding, and it sounded like a James Bond movie, sailing silently on fabric wings. I was intrigued. We drove up with him in his Toyota Jeep. I thought we were just going to watch, but Wilmer seemed to expect me to fly, and kitted

Hang gliding with Wilmer

24

me out with a harness and helmet. He clipped me into the control frame, and I practised lying in the harness and gripping the crossbar. Someone held a nose, and we stood together, my arm tucked under his harness. Run like hell, said Wilma, and we were off, and suddenly airborne.

There were huge cumulus clouds, and there must have been lots of lift, because we didn't lose altitude. Then Wilmer disappeared, leaving me in charge. I wasn't sure where he'd gone, and didn't dare look round. If I just

Heading for Macuto and the beach

headed out towards the sea and didn't make any radical moves, the glider would fly itself. And so it proved and we fly for a couple of hours. We were over the sea and still very high, and Wilmer had me push the control bar over and do tight turns to lose height. I suddenly realised we were getting low, and on the wrong side of the apartment blocks that line the coast road. We're going to crash, I thought. Then Wilmer took over and flew between two blocks of flats, and we were screaming into the beach, parallel to the sea, only a few feet from the ground. We're going to die, I thought. Then Wilmer flared the wing and plop we were down. I sat on a sea grape tree, too emotionally drained to move. While we'd been flying Scharlie had Wilmer's Jeep alone across the mountain and arrived to meet us. We have to do this hang gliding as soon as we get back home,

Jonathan and Frances on the Avila

Gran Sabana

December 1973 - January 1974

We went to the Gran Sabana with Hans and Ramon on our first Christmas in Venezuela soon after the dirt road to Boa Vista in Brazil had been constructed. Han's sisters came too, and we all packed into Han's yellow VW campervan. Our main aim was to climb Kukenan, the tepui or table mountain next to Roraima. Kukenan-tepui, or Matawi-tepui as it should rightly be named, is 2,680 metres (8,790 ft) high and rises about 700 metres above the surrounding savannah.

The Great Savanna is a region in southeastern Venezuela, extending into Brazil and Guyana. It is one of the most unusual landscapes in the world, featuring rivers, waterfalls, gorges, jungles, and savannahs that host a diverse array of plant species, a rich fauna, and the isolated table-top mesas locally known as tepuis. Tepui summits are 900 to 1,600 metres (3,000 to 5,200 ft) above the surrounding terrain, consisting of quartzite and quartzite arenites. The Guiana Highlands are ancient. They date from the

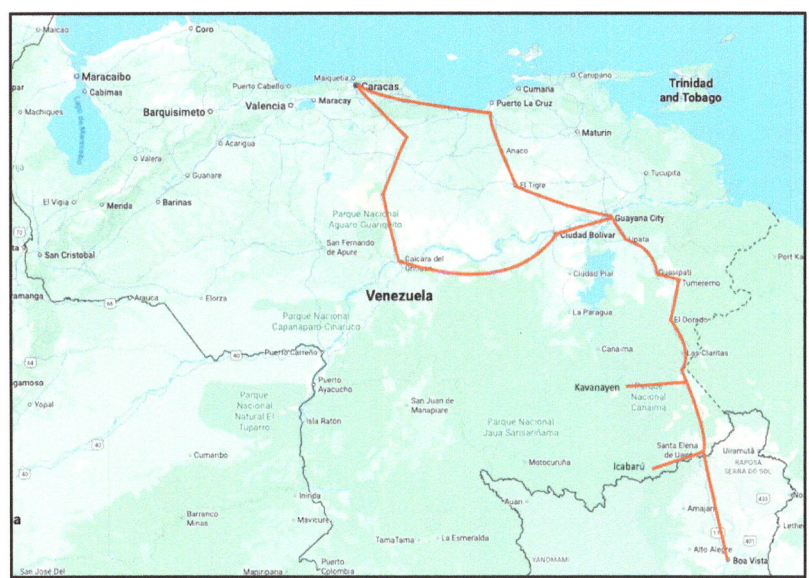

Journey to the Gran Sabana

Precambrian era, over 2 billion years ago. High precipitation combined with the long period of weathering has produced karst features that include arches, towers, tower fields, dolines, collapse shafts, polje, corridors, grikes, and large cave systems extending many kilometres.

It's a long drive from Caracas, through the plains of Anzoátegui, El Tigre and on to Ciudad Guayana. The roads back then, in 1970, weren't as good as they are today. They were single-lane, tarmacked but with large potholes that could catch you out if you were driving too fast. We passed through a series of small towns – Upata, Guasipati, Tumeremo, and finally the fabled El Dorado. This isn't the best way to appreciate these places. The roadside in Venezuela is a rich mixture of advertising hoardings, dead vehicles and rubbish, and we didn't stop and explore. Having developed without design or direction, the public face of the built environment is a combination of the worst features of American and Mediterranean lawlessness; cluttered, ugly, and anarchic. Only in private, turned in on itself, away from the dust, dirt and noise, in the patios and gardens of homes, is there tranquility and beauty.

From El Dorado, the road became increasingly difficult. At Kilometre 88,

We had to unload and push to climb La Escalera to the Gran Sabana

where La Escalera began, the road climbs 1,300 metres from the plains to the grassy plateau of the Gran Sabana. The road was a rutted, muddy wallow, and we had to unload the VW and help push. And then carry all our luggage up the hillside.

It was chilly at the Soldado Pianero, where we spent the first night. Then, it was a palm-thatched tourist shelter dedicated to the military engineers building the road from El Dorado to Santa Helena de Uairén. Later, they constructed an elaborate monument here. It was Christmas Eve and after the children had gone to sleep slept, I inflated the rubber dinghy that was their main present, and Dorothea slept in it. In the morning Frances and Jon jumped into the dingy to open their other Christmas presents.

We detoured to the mission at Kavanayén and on the way, we stopped to admire the Aponguao Falls. They are 300 feet high and one of the most beautiful in Venezuela. We met Padre Tirso, one of the Capuchin monks, dressed in his rough brown habit and hooded cowl, tied with a white woollen cord, a solar topee on his head and bare feet in sandals.

All of us shattered on getting to the plateau

Back on the main road towards Santa Helena, the Kama Falls are equally beautiful. Scharlie and I camped at the shelter here ten years later, in 1981, when we hitch-hiked to climb Ilu/Tramen Tepui.

Frances at the Aponguao Falls

Padre Tirso with Jonathan and Frances holding mango

Kama Falls

We reached San Francisco de Yuruani, where we left the family and Ramon, Hans and I set off to walk to Perai Tepui. Here we contracted Ambrosio Perez, a Pemon Indian, to guide us to Kukenan. A couple of his companions came along with a horse to carry our rucksacks and Hans's

Ambrosio and his family; Packing the horse with our kit

tent. Not that it was necessary, and it seemed overkill, since our packs were so light. But Hans insisted and it was a way of paying the community.

We walked all day across the grassland savanna. At this stage, we thought that Kukenan had not been climbed before, and that we would be

Crossing the sabana

Kukenán Tepuy (2,680 m) and Roraima (2,875 m)

Steve and Ramon resting at the Rio Kukenan

making the first ascent. It's a good day's walk to the base of the mountains. We were unsure how to approach the mountain.

The walls were imposingly steep, vertical sandstone walls. There was no path, but Ambrosio seemed sure of the way. He led us upwards towards the col between Kukenan and Roraima, the fabled table mountain to the southeast.

Ambrosio waiting for us

Salto Kukenán (674 m)

We passed below Kukenan Falls and cut a path up the most obvious way. On the cliff face itself, we took a traversing line from right to left, following a traversing ledge line. At one point, there was a scrambling mantel shelf onto a flake to get to a vegetated ledge. Near the top, there was a wide vegetated chimney to climb to the summit. We spent a chilly night sheltering under an overhanging rock.

Ramon and Hans climbing the flake

Hans, Ambrosio and Ramon on traverse

Morning after a chilly night

Steve exploring summit

The summit plateau was a bare black rock with bromeliads, some pitcher plants, heliamphora, bladderworts, and sundews, featuring sticky insect-trapping foliage. The elevation results in cooler temperatures than those of the surrounding Savannah, with frequent mists and torrential rains. This limits the type of plants that can survive the harsh climate. The weathered, craggy nature of the rock made movement difficult. After a rest and something to eat, we explored the summit. Ramon was preoccupied with the rock pools, and spent an hour or so sifting the sediment, perhaps he was looking, hoping to find gold. It's an old dream that the summits of these tepuis harbour gold and diamonds. The rivers that flow from the tepui do contain both gold and diamonds.

Ramon looking for gold and diamonds in the shallow summit pools

Ramon, Hans and Ambrosio packing to descend

Early European explorers were obsessed with legends of El Dorado, the Golden City, near the fabled Parime lake. Most famously, Sir Walter Raleigh mounted two expeditions, in 1595 and 1617, and navigated deep into the Gran Sabana via the Orinoco and Caroní Rivers. He failed to find gold and paid for this failure with his life when King James I executed him in 1618. Raleigh had journeyed as far as Roraima, and on the way, may have passed near the town of Callao on the bank of the Yuruari River. The town has been a gold-mining centre since 1853, and between 1860 and 1883 over a million ounces were exported. Diamonds are also often found with gold-bearing minerals.

In 2023, gold production was approximately 50 tons, and the illicit mining industry generated at least $3 billion per year. Despite being banned in the national parks, mining is widespread in protected areas. This results in severe contamination, deforestation, and mercury poisoning of the rivers. Ramon didn't find any gold or diamonds.

On the way back, we stopped by the river and sat, resting on the rocks by the stream. We reached Perai Tepui and met Ambrosio's family. We were treated to the local brew, cachiri, served in a communal aluminium pan that we passed round. Cachiri is a pink alcoholic drink made from fermented yucca (manioc). The women prepare it by masticating the yucca, spitting it into a gourd, and allowing it to ferment for several days. Yucca is also used for making cassava, the bread that is the staple food of the Pemon Indians, and is also the job of the women. I felt slightly queasy taking the pan and quaffing my share, but it wasn't unpleasant. Pink and somewhat sweet, and on an empty stomach, mildly intoxicating.

Kukenan is 2680 meters high and about three kilometres long. Northwest of Roraima, the Kukenan falls at 629 meters, is the tenth-highest waterfall in the world. Our ascent was in 1972. I learnt sometime later that it was climbed in 1963 as part of an expedition from Bangor University. Ambrosio knew the way because he had been on this expedition and was familiar with the route. Kukenan was closed to climbers in 1997 on safety and environmental grounds.

Hans drinking cachire, mildly alcoholic drink made from yuca

Pemon children

From Santa Helena, reunited with the family, we drove west to the mining town of Icabaru. This is one of the centres of illegal gold mining. The town had the air of the wild west, with tough-looking, unshaven men with guns lounging on street corners. We didn't linger but drove back to Santa Helena, where we met Padre Tirso again at the mission. We also made friends with a Señor Buckley and his wife, who ran a restaurant in the centre.

Padre Tirso with Dorothea, Jonathan and Hans' sister in Santa Helena

Hans wanted to see if we could reach Boa Vista on the Rio Branco, a tributary of the Rio Negro and Amazon in Brazil. The road was being constructed to reach Manaus, but by 1972, this was as far as the new highway had progressed. It had been built to transport timber from the Amazon to markets in North America, and we saw plenty of evidence of massive trunks of mahogany and other tropical hardwoods on enormous lorry trailers. I don't remember much of the journey across endless flat grassland with low trees, lagoons, ponds, and tricky river crossings.

From the Gran Sabana we drove back north via Ciudad Guyana. We stopped the night near the vast Llovizna Falls on the Caroni River near its confluence with the Orinoco. We also visited the Guri Dam and were able to drive across it, something that is now not possible. Rather than return to Caracas the same way through El Tigre and Barcelona, Hans wanted to explore the road to Caicara south of the Orinoco. It was 475 km and, back then, the road was unpaved and hot and dusty in the back of the VW. This is agricultural cattle country and we drove through coarse-grass meadows with stringy horned cattle and patches of forest by streams.

Llovizna Falls, Caroni River

Guri Dam, Caroni River

We passed through parched settlements with little to recommend them to the traveller other than their evocative names – Maripa, La Soledad, Culebra. There was a rickety wooden bridge across Rio Cuchivero and we all climbed out of the van and let Hans drive across on his own in case the structure collapsed into the river. At Caicara del Orinoco, there was a large ferry pontoon that pottered about 5 km upriver to Cabruta, where we took the main road north, another 500 km through the llanos and Valle de Pascua. The road trip from Santa Helena to Caracas via Caicara was 1,600 km (nearly 1,000 miles), much of which was on dirt roads. In all, we must have driven nearly 4,000 km. The back of a crowded old VW van was not the most comfortable way to travel, and it must have taken us a number of days, but I don't remember it being much of a hardship.

Guri Dam, with Jonathan and Frances

Dusty settlements on the road south

Sailing the VW camper van on an oil drum raft

Hans and the campervan

Road crossing the border into Brazil

Raft across river

Typical settlement

Our Wiley's jeep on second trip to Gran Sabana

Typical stretch of road

We reach Boa Vista

Crossing the Rio Orinoco on the return

Caicara del Orinoco

San Juan de los Morros

August 1972 - June 1975

We first went climbing at San Juan de los Morros in August 1972. Three roped parties climbed on Morro 2. They were me and Archie Cockburn; Hans and Wolfi, and Ramon and two of his friends, Ralf and Gundi. We called the route El Llanero. The cliffs are steep walls, but there are plenty of holds, some of them largish jugs, and when we there the rock was pristine and unpolished. We felt like pioneers and that the routes we were climbing were first ascents.

San Juan de los Morros is the gateway to the Llanos, or central plains of Venezuela. It gets its name from the five or six limestone pillars, or Morros, to the north west of the town. In the Cretaceous period, approximately 80 million years ago, they were part of a coral reef. They were uplifted into their present tooth-like form by the collision of the South American and Caribbean tectonic plates, which also formed the coastal range of the Avila. They were declared a national monument in 1949. The town is also

San Juan de los Morros

famous for the sulphurous waters of the thermal baths. President Antonio Guzmán Blanco constructed the first road to the city, enabling access to these springs.

The faro on top of the highest Morro, Morro Paurario, was constructed by an Austrian alpinist and engineer, Carlos Blashetz and was something of an engineering feat. This involved first climbing the Morro. The lighthouse was commissioned by President Juan Vicente Gómez, and inaugurated in 1929 to coincide with Gómez's birthday and the anniversary of the Battle of Carabobo. Ostensibly, it was built to act as a beacon for planes flying into the city of Maracay, which served as his capital.

We returned two or three times. In September, Hans, Ramon and I climbed the Southeast face of Morro Paurario and climbed up the steel tower into the lighthouse itself. We also did a harder climb on the arete of Morro 3 which we called La Burla (The Jest). In May 1973 I did a hard climb on Morro 1 to the right of a large yellow overhang, again with Archie Cockburn, that we called Comeback. Hans and Ramon did a climb to the right we called Black and White, after their names – Blanco and Schwarzer. My last visit was in June 1975, just before returning to England.

*Morro del Fara (*Morro Paurario,*)*

Vegetation one has to bettle through to reach the rock

Morro Grande on the right

I climbed a new route on Morro I with Hugo and Kike Arnal that we called El Monstruo because one pitch involved pulling on a grotesque gargoyle protruding from the overhanging wall.

Climbing at San Juan de los Morros was thirsty work, and we used to take a large ice-box of Polar beer in bottles and quaff them when we got down from the climbs. We only scratched the surface of the possible climbing and there are likely to be dozens of climbs and I imagine the climbing scene has developed in the last 50 years.

Steve after a day's climbing

Cueva del Guácharo

I went to the Cueva del Guácharo with Wilmer in 1974 or 1975. He told me he'd spent a month in the cave in 1967. He was a medical student interested in the effects of sensory deprivation. He had explored the whole system and wanted to show me what he'd found. I didn't give it much thought at the time, and I didn't appreciate that the invitation was important. I was up for any exploration or adventurous trip. Only recently did I realise what a privilege this was.

The Cueva del Guácharo is near the town of Caripe in Monagas State, eastern Venezuela. The cave is a limestone cavern over 10 km (6.2 mi) long, with numerous large chambers and spectacular rock formations. The name refers to the Guácharo, or Oil-bird, a nocturnal fruit-eating bird about the size of a wood pigeon in the UK. The floor of the first few hundred metres of the cave is covered in an organic layer of guano and regurgitated seeds. The cave was designated as Venezuela's first National

Stalactites Cueva del Guacharo

Monument in 1949. Alexander von Humboldt visited the cave in 1799. He described how the local Indians, the Chaimas, enter the cavern once a year to hunt oil-birds for their meat and, more importantly, for the oil they sold to the Capuchin and Franciscan missionaries for their lamps. Humboldt's somewhat florid account ended, 'We were glad to be beyond the hoarse cries of the birds, and to leave a place where darkness does not offer even the charm of silence and tranquillity'.

Salón de Humboldt

While searching online, I found a doctoral thesis by Maria Alejandra Perez, Wilmer's daughter. It was about cave exploration in Venezuela, focusing on the Cueva del Guacharo. I was impressed by the detailed maps of the cave drawn by members of the Venezuelan Speleological Society, including Wilmer. This must have been the most painstaking work, involving precise measurements of distances and angles, using a tape, compass and clinometer. I was particularly intrigued that a map was assigned a confidence level, based on the perceived accuracy of the survey.

The thesis had lengthy accounts of the disputes between key figures in the Society and the wider speleological community. The disputes were about admitting younger members into the Society, for example, Wilmer and Garbisu, the high school student who had been with Wilmer in the month-long vigil. In essence, this was a dispute about the nature of society, between individual ego and collective, cooperative action. Charles Brewer, whom I knew from my time in Venezuela, felt slighted that the Society had not adequately acknowledged his exploration of the Autana caves and Sarisariñama with David Nott. The SVE objected to him naming the larger Sarisariñama pit 'Brewer'.

Maria Alejandra describes a delightful episode during Wilmer's month in the cave. She writes that the casual conversation between the two was most likely about girlfriends. Garbisu had just broken up with his sweetheart and Wilmer could hardly contain his excitement about his new girlfriend, Mirza Pesquera, whom he met in medical school. Mirza convinced her family to visit Wilmer during his stay underground. Along with her brother, sister, her sister's boyfriend, and cave guide Benjamín Magallanes, she trekked through the cavern, through the submerged Paso de Viento, to reach Wilmer's camp. Mirza brought two cans of tropical fruit. Wilmer didn't open them for several days. Garbisu complained that Wilmer was fetishising the cans because she'd touched them.

I searched in vain in the thesis for detailed descriptions of the rock formations I'd seen. I wanted to refresh my memory. I remembered them as amazing and exceptional, quite different and more spectacular than anything I'd seen in the caves in England. I never considered myself a speleologist, but I had caved a little in the limestone of North Wales with Macolm Hodgins. I went with an old-fashioned bicycle lamp strapped to my forehead with my gabardine mac belt. I had been through tight squeezes and difficult passages, so I was not worried in any way about going with Wilmer. The thesis was erudite and interesting but lacked the wonder and excitement I'd experienced with Wilmer.

It was clear that Wilmer had taken me way beyond the present tourist section of the cave. Unfortunately, the text on the maps of the cave in the thesis I'd downloaded was challenging to read. The first 800 metres of the tourist section of the cave have incredible formations of stalagmites and stalactites, but the real wonder is beyond, in the 10 kilometres of passages. I remember great pink and cream curtains of rock hanging from the vault like giant slices of bacon. They were so thin and delicate that the light from a torch shone through them. There was a long tunnel, completely encased in sparkling diamonds. It felt like a sacrilege to walk on the floor of this magical cavern when, despite one's best efforts to step lightly, each footstep destroyed a part of the magic. And the most amazing salon of all was a place where the floor was entirely covered in delicate translucent goblets like hundreds of upturned champagne glasses.

Searching on the computer-generated version of the cave map in the thesis, I realised that these two last galleries were in the very farthest section of the cave and were named the Galeria Rio de Hielo and the Salon de las Copas. Wilmer not only showed me the secret wonders of the cave but also took me to the heart of his philosophy of scientific exploration and adventure. The wondrous things I'd seen had been formed over millions of years by the slow action of dripping water. And they could be destroyed in an instant by my incautious tread. I hope they are still there as pristine as when I saw them 50 years ago.

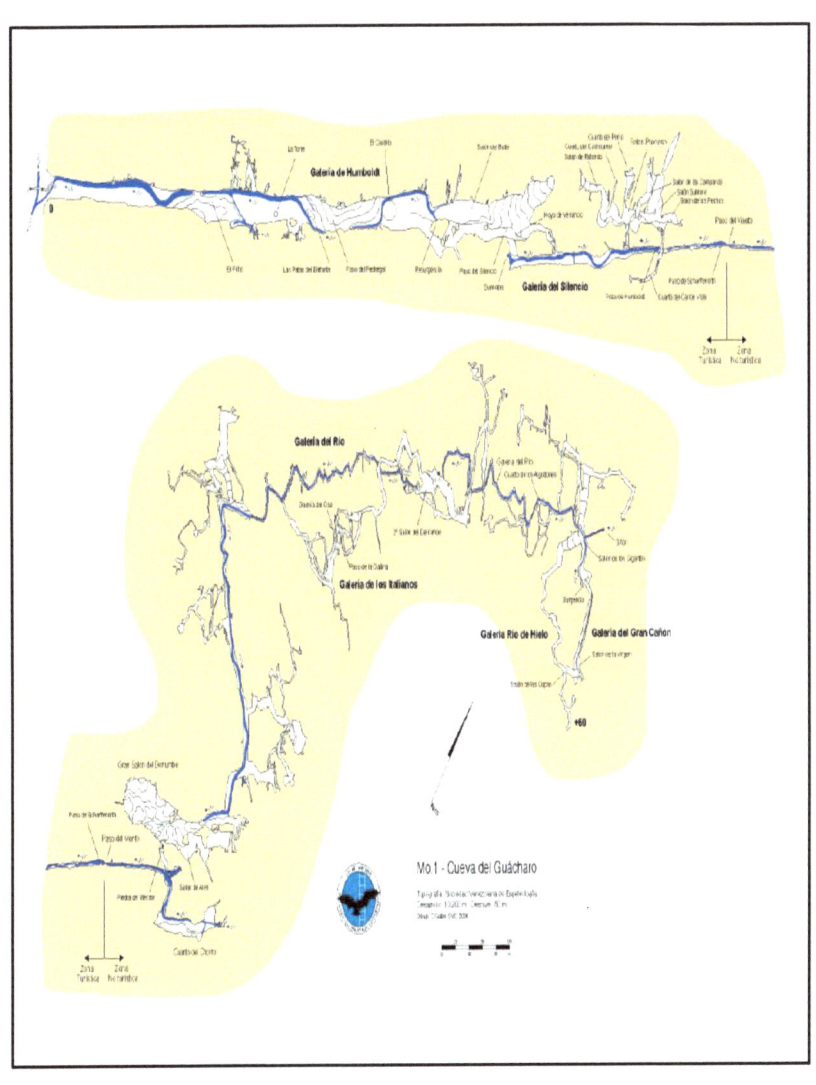

Map of 10 km of Cueva del Guacharo

Pico Bolivar and Merida

Pico Bolivar is the highest mountain in Venezuela at just under 5,000 metres. It is in Cordillera de Merida, a southern branch of Venezuelan Andes, formed about 50 million years ago by the uplift of the Nazca, Caribbean ad South America tectonic plates. To get there was a 14-hour 900-kilometre drive from Caracas to Merida. A couple of times I flew with the Venezuelan airline, Aeropostal.

Merida has the Teleferico, the world's highest and longest cable car. It was built by the military dictator, Perez Jimenez, and was completed in 1958. The teleferico went from Barinitas station in Merida at 1,577 metres to Pico Espejo at 4,765 metres, which meant you gained 3,200 metres (over 10,000 feet) in 45 minutes. The first time I went up I got a headache from the altitude sickness.

I first went to Merida with Hans and Ramon to climb Pico Bolivar by the Vinci Route. In the early 70's there were still substantial glaciers on Pico Bolivar and Pico Humboldt. I also later with Carlos Reyes, a gifted young

Pico Bolivar (4,978 m)

Venezuelan, and Bill Bostick, an American to climb the Vertigo. It was an easy scramble down from Pico Espejo to the Nido de Aguila spur. When arrived late in the afternoon and bivouacked here on the snow. My old down sleeping bag was inadequate. I had a small piece of cured pork loin called lomo embuchado, and each time I woke shaking with cold, I cut a slice a chewed it and the food provided sufficient energy to go off to sleep.

From here it was an easy walk to the base of the north face of Pico Bolivar. In the early 70's the glacier covered much of the face and the ice climb was straightforward, and there was no stone fall. The scramble to the Ventana, the col where the normal route ascends from the south side, was the most difficult part of the climb, but we found it easy.

We had arranged to meet Jorge la Riva and a party from the Centró Excursionista Caracas on the Glacier Timoncetos on the south side of the mountain and guide them up the Weiss route. This was named after Dr Franz Weiss who reached the summit in 1936. This is the first undisputed ascent of the mountain. Although an easy climb it nevertheless needed ropes. The ascent is via a chimney and couloir with a final rocky scramble

Teleferico to Pico Espejo (4,880 m)

Vinci Route, north face Pico Bolivar

to the summit where there is a large brass bust of Simon Bolivar. Apparently, it was made by Marcos Leon Mariño and placed there in 1953 by climbers from the Club Andino Venezolano and the Centró Excursionista Caracas. I didn't quite realise at the time that this was, perhaps, a big deal for Jorge and the others because I remember they were most appreciative.

In 1974 I climbed the left had arete of the Vertigo, the sharp pointed peak between Pico Espejo and Pico Bolivar. This was with Carlos Reyes and Bill Bostick. We thought it was a first ascent, but I later learnt that in 1963 David Nott had climbed the same route with George Band, who had been on the 1953 successful Everest expedition and who climbed Kangchenjunga in 1955 with Joe Brown. The two also climbed the south-west face of the Abanico. Another time Bill Bostick and I tried a direct ascent of the north face of the Vertigo, but only got up the first pitch before we abseiled off. I may have been intimidated by how steep it was.

By 2012, the glaciers on Pico Bolivar had disappeared, and by 2024, the Pico Humboldt glacier had also disappeared, making Venezuela one of the first countries to lose all its glaciers. Pico Bolivar is still snow-covered in

Vertigo spire

winter, but the permanent snow and ice has gone.

We also went to Merida as a family. We drove in the LandRover from Apartaderos and camped next to Laguna Negro, near Mucuchies. Frances remembers that she and Jon went boating in their rubber dinghy while I climbed a mountain. Another time we were staying with other families with young children in friend's house in El Valle, a suburb above Merida. We were looking after the children and playing frisbee in a meadow while the women went shopping. A friend says, try one of these, handing me a mushroom the size of a jacket button. I don't do drugs, but the sun's shining, the kids are playing happily in the stream, and anyway it's too small to have any effect. Nothing happens. The mums return, we have a late lunch and I say I'll just go for a quick walk up the hill. Maybe it was La Culeta valley.

I had completely forgotten about the mushroom. The path got steeper and narrower and I started to get tired. In the meadows there were lots of ways to go. Now there was only two, to go on or go back, both equally depressing. It's a metaphor for life. I ask a trailing vine for help and realise the mushroom's worked after all. I lay down for a rest. The ground was

Carlos Reyes on left edge of Vertigo

warm and I watched an ant climb a grass stem. Far out!

I could hear a waterfall. The sound is musical and seductive. I decided to find it. It became the reason for the climb. But when I reach it, it was only a tiny stream bubbling over stones. It's wearing away the mountain, how sad! I looked at my watch. I'd been climbing for six hours. I could climb two thousand feet an hour, so how far had I come? If a two-foot piddle can sound like a cataract, how long is a piece of string.

The birds had stopped singing; it was getting dark and there was a sense of foreboding. Suddenly I was struck violently in the chest and knocked to the ground. I opened my eyes. I was in a vast ribbed hall and thought I must have died. Then I realised that the skeletal ribs holding the roof were dead leaves and that a branch of bamboo had sprung up and hit me like a garden rake.

I was tired but the ridge started to descend. Great, I could carry on, going down. Then it climbed again and I kept going. Up and up. The vegetation thinned, and I knew I was getting near the top. That's it. That's the purpose. To reach the top, to achieve something. At the top there'll

Carlos Reyes, Bill Bostick and Steve at Pico Espejo

be lots of ways to go and there'll be no more of this agony of tired limbs and lack of breath. It'll be paradise.

It was dark so I broke off branches and overturned the pitcher plants so I could find my way back. But the plateau ended in jagged black cliffs. I think they may have been the Barro Negro and Pan de Azucar. I could climb them, but by now the effects of the mushroom were wearing off and I realised it was late and they would be worried. I resigned myself to not getting to the top. There was no purpose to the journey, no meaning to life. It had all been a waste of time. I turned round to retrace my steps and directly across the valley, in the light of a cartwheel moon, I could see twin snow-covered peaks, Pico Bolivar and Pico Espejo. It took another four hours to get back. I sat on a rock by the stream outside the house and bathed my sore feet before going in to make my peace for staying out so late.

Picnic with Dorothea, Frances and Jerry's wife Marta, Merida

www.ingramcontent.com/pod-product-compliance
Lightning Source LLC
Chambersburg PA
CBHW061030180426
43192CB00033B/36